EFFORTLE

DASH DIET COOKBOOK

Eva Evans

LEGAL & DISCLAIMER

The information contained in this book and its contents is not designed to replace or take the place of any form of medical or professional advice; and is not meant to replace the need for independent medical, financial, legal, or other professional advice or services, as may be required. The content and information in this book has been provided for educational and entertainment purposes only.

The content and information contained in this book has been compiled from sources deemed reliable, and it is accurate to the best of the Author's knowledge, information, and belief. However, the Author cannot guarantee its accuracy and validity and cannot be held liable for any errors and/or omissions. Further, changes are periodically made to this book as and when needed. Where appropriate and/or necessary, you must consult a professional (including but not limited to your doctor, attorney, financial advisor, or such other professional advisor) before using any of the suggested remedies, techniques, or information in this book.

Upon using the contents and information contained in this book, you agree to hold harmless the Author from and against any damages, costs, and expenses, including any legal fees potentially resulting from the application of any of the information provided by this book. This disclaimer applies to any loss, damages or injury caused by the use and application, whether directly or indirectly, of any advice or information presented, whether for breach of contract, tort, negligence, personal injury, criminal intent, or under any other cause of action. You agree to accept all risks of using the information presented inside this book.

You agree that by continuing to read this book, where appropriate and/or necessary, you shall consult a professional (including but not limited to your doctor, attorney, or financial advisor or such other advisor as needed) before using any of the suggested remedies, techniques, or information in this book.

TABLE OF CONTENTS

DESCRIPTION

«Effortless DASH Diet Cookbook» not only presents a diverse selection of tantalizing low-sodium recipes but also serves as a comprehensive guide to the renowned DASH (Dietary Approaches to Stop Hypertension) diet. Widely acclaimed for its effectiveness in lowering blood pressure and promoting overall health, the DASH diet emphasizes the reduction of unhealthy fats, refined sugars, and sodium intake while encouraging the consumption of nutrient-rich whole foods.

In adherence to the DASH principles, this cookbook offers a plethora of food options ranging from vibrant vegetables and succulent fruits to nourishing fat-free dairy products, lean meats, and wholesome grains. By prioritizing whole, unprocessed foods and eschewing processed foods, simple sugars, and packaged snacks, the DASH diet not only fosters better health but also redefines your palate, gradually diminishing the allure of processed junk foods.

Moreover, the DASH diet advocates for the moderation of red meat consumption, further aligning with heart-healthy dietary guidelines and promoting sustainable dietary habits. By adhering to this dietary approach, individuals with a familial predisposition to heart disease or those at risk of type-2 diabetes can effectively manage hypertension and facilitate weight loss while enhancing overall well-being.

«Effortless DASH Diet Cookbook» serves as a beacon of culinary inspiration and nutritional wisdom, guiding readers on a transformative journey towards a healthier lifestyle. With its delectable recipes and mindful eating strategies, this cookbook empowers individuals to make informed dietary choices and cultivate lifelong habits that promote vitality and longevity. Embark on the path to better health and culinary delight with «Effortless DASH Diet Cookbook» as your trusted companion.

CONQUER HIGH BLOOD PRESSURE WITH DASH DIET

The DASH diet, short for «Dietary Approaches to Stop Hypertension,» is a go-to plan for folks aiming to bring down their blood pressure. It's all about loading up on good stuff like fruits, veggies, whole grains, and lean meats.

So, why did high blood pressure become such a big deal? Well, experts quickly figured out that our love affair with fast and processed foods was a major culprit. We've been chomping down on these unhealthy options, ditching the wholesome stuff for the sake of convenience. The DASH diet swoops in to rescue us, steering us back to healthier choices.

With DASH, you'll be saying bye-bye to processed foods and hello to a bounty of fruits and veggies. Plus, it nudges you towards better proteins like fish, chicken, and beans.

But here's the real game-changer: cutting down on sodium. Processed foods are loaded with the stuff, and by ditching them, you'll significantly slash your sodium intake, which is key for lowering blood pressure.

Now, there are two versions of the DASH diet, depending on how much your blood pressure needs a reset: the Standard DASH Diet and the Lower-Sodium DASH Diet. We'll dive into the details later, but for now, just know that both revolve around whole foods and keeping that sodium in check.

Adapting to this might take a minute because, let's be real, our taste buds are used to the salty stuff. But give it a week or two, and you'll adjust just fine.

So, what's the payoff? Well, blood pressure measures how hard your blood is pushing against your blood vessels. There are two numbers: systolic pressure (when your heart beats) and diastolic pressure (when your heart's at rest). Normal is around 120/80. Anything 140/90 or higher is high blood pressure.

Now, here's the cool part: the DASH diet can help lower blood pressure, even if you're already healthy or if you don't lose weight on the plan (though many folks do shed pounds). And guess what? The less sodium you consume, the bigger the drop in blood pressure. Bottom line: DASH is your ticket to a healthier blood pressure.

DASH DIET: YOUR KEY TO WEIGHT LOSS SUCCESS

In the quest for shedding pounds, the DASH (Dietary Approaches to Stop Hypertension) diet emerges as a formidable ally. Initially devised to tackle high blood pressure, this dietary approach has garnered attention for its remarkable ability to aid weight loss. Here's how it works:

The cornerstone of the DASH diet lies in its emphasis on nutrient-rich foods and the judicious exclusion of processed junk. Picture this: vibrant fruits, crisp vegetables, hearty whole grains, and lean proteins taking center stage, while sugary snacks, greasy fried foods, and calorie-laden treats get sidelined. By opting for these wholesome options, you're not just nourishing your body; you're also priming it for weight loss.

But the magic of the DASH diet goes beyond mere food choices. It's about recalibrating your relationship with calories. By opting for nutrient-dense fare, you naturally consume fewer calories while still feeling satisfied. Think about it: a colorful salad bursting with veggies and grilled chicken leaves you feeling full and content, without the guilt or excess calories of a fast-food burger.

Moreover, the DASH diet champions the power of protein and fiber, the dynamic duo of satiety. Foods rich in these nutrients keep hunger at bay, preventing mindless snacking and overeating. And let's not forget about the healthy fats – olive oil drizzled over a salad or a handful of nuts for a snack – not only do they add flavor, but they also support overall health and well-being.

So, as you embark on your weight loss journey with the DASH diet, remember: it's not just about what you eat, but how you eat. By embracing nutrient-rich foods, moderating your calorie intake, and prioritizing satiety, the DASH diet paves the way for sustainable weight loss and a healthier, happier you.

UNLOCKING DASH DIET BENEFITS

Expounding on the Potential Health Benefits of the DASH Diet: By now, we're well aware of the DASH Diet's primary aim of lowering blood pressure. But what sets it apart from other dietary approaches? The answer lies in its multifaceted impact on various health concerns. Beyond its renowned blood pressure-lowering effects, the DASH Diet offers a host of additional benefits:

Combatting Hypertension:
A fundamental aspect contributing to the DASH diet's acclaim is its adeptness at reducing sodium intake, indirectly addressing hypertension. Sodium plays a pivotal role in regulating fluid balance within the body, with elevated levels correlating to heightened blood pressure.

Fighting Obesity:
A balanced and nutritious diet yields dual benefits for the body: it revs up metabolism, facilitating the breakdown of accumulated fat reserves, and encourages weight loss. With its emphasis on fiber-rich and low-fat foods, the DASH diet can contribute to shedding excess pounds when adhered to diligently, complemented by regular exercise.

Enhancing Heart Health:
Many cardiovascular conditions stem from the buildup of fatty deposits within arteries, veins, or heart valves, impeding blood flow and straining the heart. By targeting the root cause and curbing fat intake, the DASH diet not only mitigates the risk of heart disease but also fosters overall heart health.

Improving Kidney Function:
The kidneys play a crucial role in maintaining the body's delicate fluid balance by regulating potassium and sodium levels.

Disruption of this balance can lead to hypertension, where high sodium levels result in increased fluid retention and elevated blood pressure. The DASH diet emerges as a powerful tool in addressing this issue by advocating for reduced sodium intake, thereby supporting optimal kidney function and blood pressure management.

Combatting Diabetes:
A diet low in empty carbohydrates can effectively lower blood sugar levels, thereby reducing the risk of diabetes. Individuals with type II diabetes often experience insulin deficiency, the hormone responsible for regulating blood sugar levels. By minimizing sugar intake, the DASH diet offers significant support to those managing diabetes, helping to stabilize blood sugar levels and promote overall health.

Protecting Against Osteoporosis:
The DASH diet, rich in potassium, calcium, and protein, serves as a formidable defense against osteoporosis, a condition characterized by the weakening and deterioration of bone structure. Particularly prevalent among middle-aged women and older individuals, osteoporosis can be mitigated through consistent adherence to the DASH diet, which helps maintain optimal calcium and potassium balance essential for bone health.

Cancer Prevention:
Antioxidants play a crucial role in neutralizing harmful free radicals and reducing the risk of cancer. Thanks to its abundance of vitamins, fiber, and antioxidants, the DASH diet emerges as a potent ally in cancer prevention. By incorporating a variety of nutrient-rich foods, the DASH diet supports overall health and well-being, offering protection against the development and progression of cancer.

By embracing the principles of the DASH diet, individuals can not only enhance kidney function, manage diabetes, and protect against osteoporosis but also significantly reduce the risk of cancer, underscoring its multifaceted benefits for overall health and wellness.

BALANCED DIET BLUEPRINT: NOURISHING CHOICES

Foods to Include:

Vegetables: Incorporate a variety of vegetables into your diet, such as leafy greens (spinach, kale, lettuce), tomatoes, carrots, broccoli, zucchini, peppers, onions, garlic, and pumpkin. They are rich in vitamins, minerals, and antioxidants.

Fruits: Enjoy a variety of fruits, including berries, apples, pears, bananas, oranges, grapefruits, peaches, apricots, and grapes. They are also excellent sources of vitamins and nutrients.

Grains: Include whole grains in your diet, such as oats, barley, corn, rice, buckwheat, and wheat. They contain essential nutrients, including dietary fiber.

Legumes: Consume various types of legumes, such as beans, chickpeas, lentils, and peas. They are rich in plant-based protein, iron, potassium, and other nutrients.

Low-fat Dairy Products: Incorporate skim milk, yogurt, kefir, and cottage cheese into your diet. They are a source of calcium, protein, and vitamins.

Fish and Seafood: Prefer lean types of fish, such as salmon, cod, mackerel, and herring. They contain beneficial omega-3 fatty acids.

Nuts and Seeds: Include nuts like almonds, walnuts, hazelnuts, and seeds like flaxseeds, chia seeds, and sunflower seeds. They are rich in healthy fats, protein, vitamins, and minerals.

Foods to Limit or Avoid:

Salty Foods: Limit consumption of salty snacks, canned foods, processed meats, and salty cheeses to prevent an increase in blood pressure.

High-calorie and fatty foods: Limit consumption of fatty dairy products, fried foods, fast food, sweets, and potato chips to prevent weight gain and high cholesterol levels.

Sugary Drinks: Avoid consumption of sugary sodas, juices with added sugar, sports drinks, and energy drinks, as they contain a high amount of sugar and empty calories.

High-sugar Foods: Limit consumption of sweet desserts, candies, pastries, and other high-sugar foods to prevent sharp spikes in blood sugar levels and weight gain.

Trans Fats: Avoid foods containing trans fats, such as fried foods, fast snacks, and fried cookies, as they raise cholesterol levels and increase the risk of cardiovascular diseases.

Remember that maintaining a balanced and varied diet is crucial for a healthy lifestyle. Following the recommendations of the DASH diet will help you achieve this goal and improve your overall health.

BREAKFAST RECIPES

BLUEBERRY MUFFINS

Cooking Difficulty: 2/10	Cooking Time: 27 minutes	Servings: 12

INGREDIENTS

- ¼ c. pure maple syrup
- 2 c. blueberries
- 1 tsp. vanilla extract
- ½ tsp. baking soda
- 2 c. almond flour
- 2 tsps. baking powder
- 1 tsp. apple cider vinegar
- 2 tsps. cinnamon powder
- ½ c. walnuts, chopped
- 2 bananas, peeled and mashed
- 1 c. almond milk
- ¼ c. coconut oil, melted

STEP 1
In a bowl, combine the bananas with the almond milk, vanilla, and the other ingredients and whisk well.

STEP 2
Divide the mix into 12 muffin tins and bake at 350 degrees F for 25 minutes.

STEP 3
Serve the muffins for breakfast.

NUTRITIONAL INFORMATION
Calories 180, Fat 5g, Carbs 31g, Protein 4g

SCONES WITH NUTS AND FRUITS

Cooking Difficulty: 2/10	Cooking Time: 15 minutes	Servings: 8

INGREDIENTS

- 2 tbsps. stevia
- ¼ c. cranberries, dried
- ¼ c. walnuts, chopped
- ½ tsp. baking soda
- 1 egg, whisked
- ¼ c. apricots, chopped
- ¼ c. sunflower seeds
- 2 c. almond flour
- ¼ c. sesame seeds

STEP 1
In a bowl, combine the flour with the baking soda, cranberries, and the other ingredients and stir well.

STEP 2
Shape a square dough, roll onto a floured working surface and cut into 16 squares.

STEP 3
Arrange the squares on a baking sheet lined with parchment paper and bake the scones at 350 degrees F for 12 minutes.

STEP 4
Serve the scones for breakfast.

NUTRITIONAL INFORMATION
Calories 238, Fat 19.2g, Carbs 8.6g, Protein 8.8g

BANANA COOKIES

 Cooking Difficulty: 2/10	Cooking Time: 17 minutes	Servings: 12

INGREDIENTS

- 2 c. oats, gluten-free
- ¼ c. stevia
- 1 tsp. cinnamon powder
- 1 tsp. vanilla extract
- ½ c. raisins
- 1 c. almond butter
- 2 bananas, peeled and mashed
- 1 c. almonds, chopped

STEP 1
In a bowl, combine the butter with the stevia and the other ingredients and stir well using a hand mixer.

STEP 2
Scoop medium moulds of this mix on a baking sheet lined with parchment paper and flatten them a bit.

STEP 3
Cook them at 325 degrees F for 15 minutes and serve for breakfast.

NUTRITIONAL INFORMATION
Calories 280, Fat 16g, Carbs 29g, Protein 8g

PEACHES AND CREAM

Cooking Difficulty: 2/10	Cooking Time: 20 minutes	Servings: 4

INGREDIENTS

- 1 tsp. cinnamon
- cooking spray
- 2 c. coconut cream
- 4 peaches, sliced

STEP 1
Grease a baking pan with the cooking spray and combine the peaches with the other ingredients inside.

STEP 2
Bake this at 360 degrees F for 20 minutes, divide into bowls and serve for breakfast.

NUTRITIONAL INFORMATION
Calories 338, Fat 29.2g, Carbs 21g, Protein 4.2g

PECAN AND ORANGE BOWLS

 Cooking Difficulty: 2/10	Cooking Time: 22 minutes	Servings: 4

INGREDIENTS

- 3 tbsps. pecans, chopped
- 2 c. orange juice
- 2 tbsps. stevia
- ¼ tsp. vanilla extract
- 1 c. oats, steel cut
- 2 tbsps. coconut butter, melted

STEP 1

Heat up a pot with the orange juice over medium heat, add the oats, the butter, and the other ingredients, whisk, simmer for 20 minutes, divide into bowls and serve for breakfast.

NUTRITIONAL INFORMATION

Calories 288, Fat 39.1g, Carbs 48.3g, Protein 4.7g

SHRIMP AND EGGS MIX

 Cooking Difficulty: 3/10	Cooking Time: 13 minutes	Servings: 4

INGREDIENTS

- 8 whisked eggs
- 1 tbsp. olive oil
- ½ lb. deveined shrimp, peeled and chopped
- ¼ c. chopped green onions
- 1 tsp. sweet paprika
- black pepper
- 1 tbsp. chopped cilantro

STEP 1
Ensure that you heat the pan; add the spring onions, toss and sauté for 2 minutes.

STEP 2
Add the shrimp, stir, then cook for 4 minutes more.

STEP 3
Add the eggs, paprika, salt, and pepper, toss, then cook for 5 minutes more.

STEP 4
Divide the mix between plates, sprinkle the cilantro on top, and serve for breakfast.

NUTRITIONAL INFORMATION
Calories 227, Fat 13.3g, Carbs 2.3g, Protein 24.2g

FRENCH TOAST

Cooking Difficulty: 2/10	Cooking Time: 13 minutes	Servings: 2

INGREDIENTS

- 1 tsp. vanilla extract
- ½ c. coconut milk
- cooking spray
- 4 bread slices, whole wheat
- 2 eggs, whisked

STEP 1

In a bowl, combine the sugar with the milk, eggs, and the vanilla and whisk well.

STEP 2

Dip each bread slice in this mix.

STEP 3

Heat up a pan greased with cooking spray over medium heat, add the French toast, cook for 2-3 minutes on each side, divide between plates and serve for breakfast.

NUTRITIONAL INFORMATION

Calories 508, Fat 30.8g, Carbs 55.1g, Protein 16.2g

BLUEBERRY & MINT PARFAITS

 Cooking Difficulty: 2/10

 Cooking Time: 5 minutes

 Servings: 4

NUTRITIONAL INFORMATION
Calories: 272, Fat: 8g, Protein: 10g, Carbs: 25g

INGREDIENTS

- 1½ c. wholegrain rolled oats
- 1 c. almond milk
- 2 c. Greek yogurt, unsweetened
- 1 c. fresh blueberries
- blackberries (optional)
- 4 freshly chopped mint leaves

STEP 1
Place the oats and almond milk into a bowl and stir together to combine (this helps the oats to soften).

STEP 2
Spoon the oat and almond milk mixture evenly into your 4 containers.

STEP 3
Place a drop of yogurt into each container on top of the oats (use half of the yogurt as you'll be adding another layer of it).

STEP 4
Divide half of the blueberries between the 4 containers and sprinkle on top of the yogurt.

STEP 5
Add another layer of yogurt and then another layer of blueberries (you can use them all up at this stage).

STEP 6
Sprinkle the fresh mint over the top of each parfait.

STEP 7
Cover and place into the fridge to store until needed!

CHIA SEED PUDDING

 Cooking Difficulty: 1/10	Cooking Time: 12 minutes	Servings: 1

INGREDIENTS

- 1/2 cup almond milk
- 2 tbsp. chia seeds
- berries

STEP 1

Combine chia seeds and milk in a large bowl. Let the mixture sit for 10 minutes, then stir again as soon as the chia seeds begin to swell.

STEP 2

Cover the bowl with a lid and refrigerate for an hour or more.

STEP 3

Stir the chia pudding before serving and add your favorite berries. Enjoy!

NUTRITIONAL INFORMATION

180 Calories, 7g Fat, 3g Carbs, 3g Protein

KIWI SPINACH SMOOTHIE

 Cooking Difficulty: 1/10

 Cooking Time: 1 minutes

 Servings: 1

INGREDIENTS

- 1 c. baby spinach
- 2 peeled kiwi, halved
- ½ c. apple juice
- 2 tbsps. flaxseed, ground
- ½ peeled banana
- 12 ice cubes

STEP 1

Using a blender, set in all your ingredients. Blend well until very smooth. Enjoy!

NUTRITIONAL INFORMATION
Calories: 284, Fat: 5.6 g, Carbs: 55.3 g, Protein: 5.9 g

STRAWBERRY YOGURT

 Cooking Difficulty: 1/10	Cooking Time: 10 minutes	Servings: 4

INGREDIENTS

- 1 c. strawberry halved
- 4 c. non-fat yogurt
- ½ tsp. vanilla extract

STEP 1

In a bowl, combine the yogurt with the strawberry, and vanilla, toss and keep in the fridge for 10 minutes. Divide into bowls and serve f breakfast.

NUTRITIONAL INFORMATION
Calories: 79, Fat: 0.4 g, Carbs: 15 g, Protein: 1.3 g

SPINACH OMELET

Cooking Difficulty: 2/10	Cooking Time: 20 minutes	Servings: 4

INGREDIENTS

- 8 whisked eggs
- 1 c. baby spinach
- black pepper
- 1 tbsp. olive oil
- 2 chopped spring onions
- 1 tsp. sweet paprika
- 1 tsp. ground cumin
- 1 tbsp. chopped chives

STEP 1
Ensure that you heat the pan; add the spring onions, paprika, and cumin, stir and sauté for 5 minutes.

STEP 2
Add the eggs, the spinach, and pepper toss spread into the pan, cover it then cook for 15 minutes.

STEP 3
Sprinkle the chives on top, divide everything between plates and serve.

NUTRITIONAL INFORMATION
Calories 345, Fat 12g, Carbs 8g, Protein 13.3g

BAKED EGGS AND ARTICHOKES

 Cooking Difficulty: 3/10	Cooking Time: 22 minutes	Servings: 4

INGREDIENTS

- 1 c. canned artichokes, unsalted drained and chopped
- 4 slices low-fat cheddar, shredded
- 1 tbsp. avocado oil
- 4 eggs
- 1 tbsp. cilantro, chopped
- 1 yellow onion, chopped

STEP 1
Grease 4 ramekins with the oil, divide the onion in each, add the artichokes and top with cilantro, crack an egg in each, and cheddar cheese.

STEP 2
Introduce the ramekins in the oven and bake at 380 degrees F for 20 minutes.

STEP 3
Serve the baked eggs for breakfast.

NUTRITIONAL INFORMATION
Calories 345, Fat 12g, Carbs 8g, Protein 13.3g

TURMERIC CHEESY SCRAMBLE

Cooking Difficulty: 3/10	Cooking Time: 17 minutes	Servings: 4

INGREDIENTS

- 1 tsp. turmeric powder
- 4 eggs, whisked
- 1 red bell pepper, chopped
- 2 shallots, chopped
- ¼ tsp. black pepper
- 3 tbsps. low-fat mozzarella, shredded
- 1 tbsp. olive oil

STEP 1

Heat up a pan with the oil over medium heat, add the shallots and the bell pepper, stir and sauté for 5 minutes.

STEP 2

Add the eggs mixed with the rest of the ingredients, stir, cook for 10 minutes, divide everything between plates and serve.

NUTRITIONAL INFORMATION
Calories 138, Fat 8g, Carbs 4.6g, Protein 12g

CHERRY BERRY SMOOTHIE

 Cooking Difficulty: 1/10	Cooking Time: 1 minutes	Servings: 2

INGREDIENTS

- 1 c. cherries
- 2 c. fresh kale
- 4 tsps. honey
- 1 c. blueberries
- 2 c. almond milk

STEP 1
Add all the listed ingredients to a blender .

STEP 2
Process well to obtain a smooth and creamy texture.

STEP 3
Serve chilled and enjoy!

NUTRITIONAL INFORMATION
Calories: 220, Fat: 2.8g, Carbs: 47.7g, Protein: 3.7g

PEACHES AND CREAM

 Cooking Difficulty: 2/10	Cooking Time: 4 minutes	Servings: 4

INGREDIENTS

- 2 c. coconut yogurt
- ½ c. water
- 1 pear, cored and chopped
- 2 tsps. pumpkin pie spice
- 2 tbsps. maple syrup
- ¼ c. cashews
- 2 c. pumpkin puree

STEP 1

In a blender, combine the cashews with the water and the other ingredients except the yogurt and pulse well.

STEP 2

Divide the yogurt into bowls, also divide the pumpkin cream on top and serve.

NUTRITIONAL INFORMATION

Calories 200, Fat 6.4g, Carbs 32.9g, Protein 5.5g

LUNCH RECIPES

BEEF AND ZUCCHINI PAN

 Cooking Difficulty: 2/10	Cooking Time: 22 minutes	Servings: 4

INGREDIENTS

- 1 tbsp. cilantro, chopped
- ½ c. yellow onion, chopped
- 1 tsp. Italian seasoning
- 14 oz. canned tomatoes, unsalted and chopped
- 1 tbsp. olive oil
- 1 tbsp. chives, chopped
- 2 garlic cloves, minced
- ¼ c. low-fat parmesan, shredded
- 1 lb. beef, ground
- 1 c. zucchini, cubed

STEP 1
Heat up a pan with the oil over medium heat, add the garlic, onion, and the beef and brown for 5 minutes.

STEP 2
Add the rest of the ingredients, toss, cook for 15 minutes more, divide into bowls, and serve for lunch.

NUTRITIONAL INFORMATION
Calories: 79, Fat: 0.4 g, Carbs: 15 g, Protein: 1.3 g

THYME BEEF AND POTATOES MIX

Cooking Difficulty: 3/10	Cooking Time: 27 minutes	Servings: 4

INGREDIENTS

- 1 c. canned tomatoes, unsalted and chopped
- 3 tbsps. olive oil
- 2 tsps. thyme, dried
- 1 ¾ lbs. red potatoes, peeled and cubed
- ¼ tsp. black pepper
- ½ lb. beef, ground
- 1 yellow onion, chopped
- olive (optional)

STEP 1
Heat up a pan with the oil over medium-high heat, add the onion and the beef, stir and brown for 5 minutes.

STEP 2
Add the potatoes and the rest of the ingredients, toss, bring to a simmer, cook for 20 minutes more, divide into bowls, and serve for lunch.

NUTRITIONAL INFORMATION
Calories 216, Fat 14.5g, Carbs 40.7g, Protein 22.2g

SHRIMP AND STRAWBERRY SALAD

Cooking Difficulty: 2/10	Cooking Time: 5 minutes	Servings: 4

INGREDIENTS

- 2 tbsps. balsamic vinegar
- 1 endive, shredded
- 2 c. strawberries halved
- 1 c. baby spinach
- 1 tbsp. lime juice
- 2 garlic cloves, minced
- 1 lb. shrimp, peeled and deveined
- 2 tbsps. olive oil
- feta cheese optional

STEP 1
Heat up a pan with the oil over medium-high heat, add the garlic and brown for 1 minute.

STEP 2
Add the shrimp and lime juice, toss and cook for 3 minutes on each side.

STEP 3
In a salad bowl, combine the shrimp with the endive, and the other ingredients, toss and serve for lunch.

NUTRITIONAL INFORMATION
Calories 260, Fat 9.7g, Carbs 16.5g, Protein 28g

CHICKEN, TOMATO, AND SPINACH SALAD

Cooking Difficulty: 2/10	Cooking Time: 3 minutes	Servings: 4

INGREDIENTS

- ¼ tsp. black pepper
- 1 red onion, chopped
- 2 rotisserie chicken, de-boned, skinless and shredded
- ¼ c. walnuts, chopped
- 1 lb. cherry tomatoes, halved
- green pea
- 2 tbsps. lemon juice
- 1 tbsp. olive oil
- 4 c. baby spinach

STEP 1

In a salad bowl, combine the chicken with the tomato and the other ingredients, toss and serve for lunch.

NUTRITIONAL INFORMATION

Calories 380, Fat 40g, Carbs 1g, Protein 17g

SHRIMP AND ASPARAGUS SALAD

Cooking Difficulty: 2/10	Cooking Time: 12 minutes	Servings: 4

INGREDIENTS

- ¼ c. raspberry vinegar
- 2 tbsps. olive oil
- 2 c. cherry tomatoes halved
- 2 lbs. shrimp, peeled and deveined
- ¼ tsp. black pepper
- 1 lb. asparagus, pre-cooked
- 1 tbsps. lemon juice

STEP 1

Heat up a pan with the oil over medium-high heat, add the shrimp, toss and cook for 2 minutes. Add the asparagus and the other ingredients, toss, cook for 8 minutes more, divide into bowls, and serve for lunch.

NUTRITIONAL INFORMATION
Calories: 79, Fat: 0.4 g, Carbs: 15 g, Protein: 1.3 g

FISH TACOS

Cooking Difficulty: 2/10	Cooking Time: 10 minutes	Servings: 2

INGREDIENTS

- 1 tbsp. tomato puree
- 1 tbsp. salsa
- 1 tbsp. light mayonnaise
- 2 cod fillets, de-boned, skinless, and cubed
- 1 tbsp. olive oil
- 1 tbsp. low-fat mozzarella, shredded
- 1 tbsp. cilantro, chopped
- 4 taco shells, whole wheat
- 1 red onion, chopped

STEP 1
Heat up a pan with the oil over medium heat, add the onion, stir and cook for 2 minutes.

STEP 2
Add the fish and tomato puree, toss gently, and cook for 5 minutes more.

STEP 3
Spoon this into the taco shells, also divide the mayo, salsa, and the cheese and serve for lunch.

NUTRITIONAL INFORMATION
Calories 466, Fat 14.5g, Carbs 56.6g, Protein 32.9g

ZUCCHINI CAKES

Cooking Difficulty: 2/10	Cooking Time: 22 minutes	Servings: 4

INGREDIENTS

- 2 tbsps. olive oil
- 2 tbsps. almond flour
- 1/3 c. carrot, shredded
- 1 tsp. lemon zest, grated
- 1 garlic clove, minced
- 1 egg, whisked
- 1/3 c. low-fat cheddar, grated
- 2 zucchinis, grated
- 1 tbsp. cilantro, chopped
- 1 yellow onion, chopped
- ¼ tsp. black pepper

STEP 1

In a bowl, combine the zucchinis with the garlic, onion, and the other ingredients except for the oil, stir well and shape medium cakes out of this mix.

STEP 2

Heat up a pan with the oil over medium-high heat, add the zucchini cakes, cook for 5 minutes on each side, divide between plates and serve with a side salad.

NUTRITIONAL INFORMATION

Calories 271, Fat 8.7g, Carbs 14.3g, Protein 4.6g

CHICKPEAS AND TOMATOES STEW

Cooking Difficulty: 3/10	Cooking Time: 22 minutes	Servings: 4

INGREDIENTS

- 1 c. low-sodium chicken stock
- 1 yellow onion, chopped
- 14 oz. canned chickpeas, unsalted, drained, and rinsed
- 2 tsps. chili powder
- ¼ tsp. black pepper
- 14 oz. canned tomatoes, unsalted and cubed
- 1 tbsp. olive oil
- 1 tbsp. cilantro, chopped

STEP 1
Heat up a pot with the oil over medium-high heat, add the onion and chili powder, stir and cook for 5 minutes.

STEP 2
Add the chickpeas and the other ingredients, toss, cook for 15 minutes over medium heat, divide into bowls and serve for lunch.

NUTRITIONAL INFORMATION
Calories 299, Fat 13.2g, Carbs 17.2g, Protein 8.1g

RICE AND BEAN BURRITOS

 Cooking Difficulty: 3/10

 Cooking Time: 20 minutes

 Servings: 8

NUTRITIONAL INFORMATION
Calories 290, Carbs 49 g, Fats 6 g, Protein 9 g

INGREDIENTS

- 32 oz. fat-free refried beans
- 6 tortillas
- 2 c. cooked rice
- ½ c. salsa
- 1 tbsp. olive oil
- 1 bunch green onions, chopped
- 2 bell peppers, chopped
- guacamole

STEP 1
Preheat the oven to 375°F.

STEP 2
Dump the refried beans into a saucepan and place over medium heat to warm.

STEP 3
Heat the tortillas and lay them out on a flat surface.

STEP 4
Spoon the beans in a long mound that runs across the tortilla, just a little off from center.

STEP 5
Spoon some rice and salsa over the beans; add the green pepper and onions to taste, along with any other finely chopped vegetables you like.

STEP 6
Fold over the shortest edge of the plain tortilla and roll it up, folding in the sides as you go.

STEP 7
Place each burrito, seam side down, on a nonstick-sprayed baking sheet.

STEP 8
Brush with olive oil and bake for 15 minutes. Serve with guacamole.

PORK CHOPS WITH MUSHROOMS

Cooking Difficulty: 3/10	Cooking Time: 490 minutes	Servings: 4

INGREDIENTS

- 1 tsp. sweet paprika
- 1 tbsp. olive oil
- 1 tbsp. rosemary, chopped
- 2 shallots, chopped
- ½ c. beef stock, low-sodium
- 1 lb. white mushrooms, sliced
- 4 pork chops
- ¼ tsp. garlic powder

STEP 1

Heat up a pan with the oil over medium-high heat, add the pork chops and the shallots, toss, brown for 10 minutes, and transfer to a slow cooker.

STEP 2

Add the rest of the ingredients, put the lid on, and cook on Low for 8 hours.

STEP 3

Divide the pork chops and mushrooms between plates and serve for lunch.

NUTRITIONAL INFORMATION

Calories 349, Fat 24g, Carbs 46.3g, Protein 17.5g

CORIANDER SHRIMP SALAD

Cooking Difficulty: 2/10	Cooking Time: 8 minutes	Servings: 4

INGREDIENTS

- 1 tbsp. coriander, chopped
- 1 lb. shrimp, deveined and peeled
- 1 red onion, sliced
- ¼ tsp. black pepper
- 2 c. baby arugula
- 1 tbsp. lemon juice
- 1 tbsp. olive oil
- 1 tbsp. balsamic vinegar

STEP 1

Heat up a pan with the oil over medium heat, add the onion, stir and sauté for 2 minutes.

STEP 2

Add the shrimp and the other ingredients, toss, cook for 6 minutes, divide into bowls and serve for lunch.

NUTRITIONAL INFORMATION

Calories 341, Fat 11.5g, Carbs 17.3g, Protein 14.3g

BLACK BEAN STUFFED SWEET POTATOES

Cooking Difficulty: 4/10	Cooking Time: 80 minutes	Servings: 4

NUTRITIONAL INFORMATION
Calories: 387, Fat: 16.1 g, Carbs: 53 g, Protein: 10.4 g

INGREDIENTS

- 4 sweet potatoes
- 15 oz. cooked black beans
- ½ tsp. ground black pepper
- ½ red onion, peeled, diced
- ¼ tsp. onion powder
- ¼ tsp. garlic powder
- ¼ tsp. red chili powder
- ¼ tsp. cumin
- 1 tsp. lime juice
- 1 ½ tbsps. olive oil
- ½ c. cashew cream sauce

STEP 1
Spread sweet potatoes on a baking tray greased with oil and bake for 65 minutes at 350 degrees f until tender.

STEP 2
Meanwhile, prepare the sauce, and for this, whisk together the cream sauce, black pepper, and lime juice until combined, set aside until required.

STEP 3
When 10 minutes of the baking time of potatoes are left, heat a skillet pan with oil. Add in onion to cook until golden for 5 minutes.

STEP 4
Then stir in spice, cook for another 3 minutes, stir in bean until combined and cook for 5 minutes until hot.

STEP 5
Let roasted sweet potatoes cool for 10 minutes, then cut them open, mash the flesh and top with bean mixture, cilantro and avocado, and then drizzle with cream sauce.

STEP 6
Serve straight away.

CABBAGE AND BEEF MIX

 Cooking Difficulty: 3/10

 Cooking Time: 22 minutes

 Servings: 4

INGREDIENTS

- ¼ tsp. red pepper, crushed
- ¼ c. beef stock, low-sodium
- ¾ c. red bell peppers, chopped
- 2 tomatoes, cubed
- ¼ c. green onions, chopped
- 2 yellow onions, chopped
- 1 lb. beef, ground
- 1 green cabbage head, shredded
- 1 tbsp. olive oil
- ¼ c. cilantro, chopped

STEP 1

Heat up a pan with the oil over medium heat, add the meat and the onions, stir and brown for 5 minutes.

STEP 2

Add the cabbage and the other ingredients, toss, cook for 15 minutes, divide into bowls and serve for lunch.

NUTRITIONAL INFORMATION
Calories 328, Fat 11g, Carbs 20.1g, Protein 38.3g

ZUCCHINI CREAM SOUP

 Cooking Difficulty: 2/10	Cooking Time: 22 minutes	Servings: 4

INGREDIENTS

- 1 tbsp. dill, chopped
- 1 yellow onion, chopped
- 1 lb. zucchinis, chopped
- 32 oz. chicken stock, low-sodium
- 1 tbsp. olive oil
- 1 c. coconut cream
- 1 tsp. ginger, grated

STEP 1

Heat up a pot with the oil over medium heat, add the onion and ginger, stir and cook for 5 minutes.

STEP 2

Add the zucchinis and the other ingredients, bring to a simmer, and cook over medium heat for 15 minutes.

STEP 3

Blend using an immersion blender, divide into bowls and serve.

NUTRITIONAL INFORMATION

Calories 293, Fat 12.3g, Carbs 11.2g, Protein 6.4g

GARLICKY KALE & PEA SAUTÉ

 Cooking Difficulty: 2/10

 Cooking Time: 8 minutes

 Servings: 2

INGREDIENTS

- 2 sliced garlic cloves
- 1 chopped hot red chile
- 2 tbsps. olive oil
- 2 bunches chopped kale
- 1 lb. frozen peas

STEP 1
In a saucepot, mix the ingredients except peas. Cook until the kale becomes tender for about 6 minutes.

STEP 2
Add peas and cook for 2 more minutes.

NUTRITIONAL INFORMATION
85 Calories, 3g Fats, 11g Net Carbs, and 5g Protein

BAKED BROCCOLI

 Cooking Difficulty: 2/10

 Cooking Time: 20 minutes

 Servings: 4

INGREDIENTS

- 2 minced garlic cloves
- 2 tbsps. olive oil
- 1 lb. broccoli florets
- ½ tsp. ground nutmeg
- ½ tsps. dried rosemary
- black pepper

STEP 1

In a roasting pan, combine the broccoli with the garlic and the other ingredients, toss and bake at 400 degrees F for 20 minutes. Divide the mix between plates and serve.

NUTRITIONAL INFORMATION

Calories 150, Fat 4.1g, Carbs 3.2g, Protein 2g

CHICKEN AND GARLIC SAUCE

 Cooking Difficulty: 3/10	Cooking Time: 22 minutes	Servings: 4

INGREDIENTS

- 1 tbsp. chives, chopped
- 1 yellow onion, chopped
- 1 lb. chicken breasts, skinless, deboned and cubed
- 2 c. coconut cream
- 4 garlic cloves, minced
- 1 tbsp. basil, chopped
- 1 c. chicken stock, low-sodium
- 1 tbsp. olive oil
- ¼ tsp. black pepper
- white mushrooms halved (optional)

STEP 1

Heat up a pan with the oil over medium-high heat, add the garlic, onion, and the meat, toss and brown for 5 minutes.

STEP 2

Add the stock and the rest of the ingredients, bring to a simmer and cook over medium heat for 15 minutes.

STEP 3

Divide the mix between plates and serve.

NUTRITIONAL INFORMATION

Calories 451, Fat 16.6g, Carbs 34.4g, Protein 34.5g

DINNER RECIPES

GINGER SESAME HALIBUT

Cooking Difficulty: 3/10	Cooking Time: 17 minutes	Servings: 3

INGREDIENTS

- 24 oz. halibut fillets
- 1½ tbsps. minced fresh ginger
- 1½ tsps. soy sauce
- ½ tsps. worcestershire sauce
- 1½ tsps. olive oil
- ¾ tsp. sesame oil
- ¾ tsp. rice wine vinegar

STEP 1
Set the oven to 400 degrees F to preheat. Line a baking sheet with aluminum foil and set aside.

STEP 2
Combine the sesame and olive oils in a bowl, then stir in the rice vinegar, soy sauce, worcestershire sauce and ginger.

STEP 3
Add the fish fillets and turn several times to coat. Arrange the fish fillets on the prepared baking sheet. Bake for 17 minutes, or until done.

STEP 4
Cover each fish fillet with aluminum foil and refrigerate for up to 3 days, or freeze for up to 2 weeks. Reheat before serving.

NUTRITIONAL INFORMATION
237 Calories, 35g Fats, 1g Net Carbs, and 33g Protein

CAULIFLOWER STEAK WITH SWEET-PEA PUREE

Cooking Difficulty: 3/10	Cooking Time: 35 minutes	Servings: 2

NUTRITIONAL INFORMATION
Calories 234, Fat 3.8g, Carbs 40.3g, Protein 14.5g

INGREDIENTS

cauliflower:
- 2 heads cauliflower
- 1 tsp. olive oil
- ¼ tsp. paprika
- 1 tsp. coriander
- ¼ tsp. black pepper

sweet-pea puree:
- 10 oz. frozen green peas
- 1 onion, chopped
- 2 tbsps. fresh parsley
- ¼ c. unsweetened soy milk

STEP 1
Preheat oven to 425F.

STEP 2
Remove bottom core of cauliflower. Stand it on its base, starting in the middle, slice in half. Then slice steaks about ¾ inches thick.

STEP 3
Using a baking pan, set in the steaks.

STEP 4
Using olive oil, coat the front and back of the steaks.

STEP 5
Sprinkle with coriander, paprika, and pepper.

STEP 6
Bake for 30 minutes, flipping once.

STEP 7
Meanwhile, steam the chopped onion and peas until soft.

STEP 8
Place these vegetables in a blender with milk and parsley and blend until smooth.

PORK WITH PEACHES MIX

Cooking Difficulty: 3/10	Cooking Time: 27 minutes	Servings: 4

INGREDIENTS

- ¼ c. veggie stock, low-sodium
- 2 peaches, pitted and sliced
- 2 tbsps. olive oil
- ¼ tsp. onion powder
- 2 lbs. pork tenderloin,
- black pepper
- ¼ tsp. smoked paprika

STEP 1
Heat up a pan with the oil over medium heat, add the meat, toss and cook for 10 minutes.

STEP 2
Add the peaches and the other ingredients, toss, bring to a simmer and cook over medium heat for 15 minutes more.

STEP 3
Divide the whole mix between plates and serve.

NUTRITIONAL INFORMATION
Calories 290, Fat 11.8g, Carbs 13.7g, Protein 24g

COCONUT PORK CHOPS

 Cooking Difficulty: 3/10

 Cooking Time: 20 minutes

 Servings: 4

INGREDIENTS

- 1 c. coconut milk
- 1 yellow onion, chopped
- ¼ c. cilantro, chopped
- 4 pork chops
- 2 tbsps. olive oil
- 1 tbsp. chili powder

STEP 1
Heat up a pan with the oil over medium-high heat, add the onion and the chili powder, toss and sauté for 5 minutes.

STEP 2
Add the pork chops and brown them for 2 minutes on each side.

STEP 3
Add the coconut milk, toss, bring to a simmer and cook over medium heat for 11 minutes more.

STEP 4
Add the cilantro, toss, divide everything into bowls, and serve.

NUTRITIONAL INFORMATION
Calories 365, Fat 7g, Fiber 6, Carbs 15.6g, Protein 32.4g

SALMON AND POTATO SALAD

 Cooking Difficulty: 3/10	Cooking Time: 20 minutes	Servings: 6

INGREDIENTS

- 1 tbsp. chopped parsley
- 6 oz. salmon
- 1 chopped onion
- 1 tbsp. olive oil
- 3 baking potatoes
- basil leaves

STEP 1
Boil the potatoes until done. While those are boiling, heat up some oil in a pan and fry the onions.

STEP 2
Place the salmon slices into a dish and put the onions on top.

STEP 3
Top with the potatoes and sprinkle the parsley on top before serving and basil leaves.

NUTRITIONAL INFORMATION
120 Calories, 3.5g Fats, 20g Net Carbs, and 2g Protein

PORK WITH CILANTRO SAUCE

 Cooking Difficulty: 3/10

 Cooking Time: 23 minutes

 Servings: 4

INGREDIENTS

- black pepper
- 2 lbs. pork stew meat,
- 1 tbsp. pine nuts
- 1 tbsp. lemon juice
- 4 tbsps. olive oil
- 1 tbsp. parmesan, fat-free and grated
- 1 c. cilantro leaves
- 1 tsp. chili powder

STEP 1

In a blender, combine the cilantro with the pine nuts, 3 tablespoons oil, parmesan, and lemon juice and pulse well.

STEP 2

Heat up a pan with the remaining oil over medium heat, add the meat, chili powder, and the black pepper, toss and brown for 5 minutes.

STEP 3

Add the cilantro sauce, and cook over medium heat for 15 minutes more, stirring from time to time.

STEP 4

Divide the pork between plates and serve right away.

NUTRITIONAL INFORMATION

Calories 270, Fat 6.6g, Carbs 12.6g, Protein 22.4g

VEGETARIAN RATATOUILLE

 Cooking Difficulty: 3/10	Cooking Time: 40 minutes	Servings: 4

INGREDIENTS

- 2 sliced red onions
- 1 sliced eggplant
- 2 sliced curettes
- 1 sliced red bell pepper
- 2 sliced squashes
- 2 c. tomato sauce
- ¼ c. parmesan cheese
- a handful of oregano & thyme

STEP 1
Set your oven to 375 F.

STEP 2
Stir the tomato sauce into a ceramic baking dish. Sprinkle the half of parmesan cheese over the sauce.

STEP 3
Pick one slice of each vegetable and line them up nicely. Arrange slices in baking dish and repeat the same order. Finish with a sprinkle of remaining parmesan cheese, and herbs.

STEP 4
Cook for 35-40 minutes until the vegetables are cooked through and a little crisp.

NUTRITIONAL INFORMATION
120 Calories, 3.5g Fats, 20g Net Carbs, and 2g Protein

SHRIMP AND PINE NUTS MIX

 Cooking Difficulty: 2/10

 Cooking Time: 11 minutes

 Servings: 4

INGREDIENTS

- 1 tbsp. thyme, chopped
- 2 tbsps. pine nuts
- black pepper
- 1 tbsp. lime juice
- 2 tbsps. chives, finely chopped
- 3 garlic cloves, minced
- 1 lb. shrimp, peeled and deveined
- 2 tbsps. olive oil

STEP 1

Heat up a pan with the oil over medium-high heat, add the garlic, thyme, pine nuts, and lime juice, toss and cook for 3 minutes.

STEP 2

Add the shrimp, black pepper, and the chives, toss, cook for 7 minutes more, divide between plates and serve.

NUTRITIONAL INFORMATION

Calories 290, Fat 13g, Carbs 13.9g, Protein 10g

PARMESAN TURKEY

 Cooking Difficulty: 3/10	Cooking Time: 26 minutes	Servings: 4

INGREDIENTS

- 2 shallots, chopped
- 1 tbsp. olive oil
- black pepper
- 1 c. coconut milk
- ½ c. low-fat parmesan, grated
- 1 lb. turkey breast, skinless, deboned and cubed

STEP 1

Heat up a pan with the oil over medium-high heat, add the shallots, toss and cook for 5 minutes. Add the meat, coconut milk, and black pepper, toss and cook over medium heat for 15 minutes more. Add the parmesan, cook for 2-3 minutes, divide everything between plates, and serve.

NUTRITIONAL INFORMATION
Calories 320, Fat 11.4g, Carbs 14.3g, Protein 11.3g

CUBED STEAK

 Cooking Difficulty: 3/10

 Cooking Time: 29 minutes

 Servings: 8

INGREDIENTS

- 1 c. water
- 8 cubed steaks
- black pepper
- 8 oz. tomato sauce
- 1/3 c. green pitted olives
- 2 tbsps. brine
- 1 red pepper
- ½ onion

STEP 1

Chop the peppers and onions into ¼-inch strips. Prepare the beef with the pepper. Toss into the Instant Pot – along with the remainder of the fixings. Secure the top and prepare for 25 minutes under high pressure. Natural release and serve.

NUTRITIONAL INFORMATION

154 Calories, 3g Carbs, 23.5g Protein, 5.5g Fat

CASHEW TURKEY MEDLEY

 Cooking Difficulty: 3/10

 Cooking Time: 23 minutes

 Servings: 4

INGREDIENTS

- 1 tbsp. cilantro, chopped
- black pepper
- 1 c. cashews, chopped
- 2 ½ tbsps. cashew butter
- ½ tbsp. olive oil
- ¼ c. chicken stock, low-sodium
- 1 yellow onion, chopped
- 1 lb. turkey breast, skinless, deboned and cubed
- ½ tsp. sweet paprika

STEP 1
Heat up a pan with the oil over medium-high heat, add the onion, stir and sauté for 5 minutes.

STEP 2
Add the meat and brown it for 5 minutes more.

STEP 3
Add the rest of the ingredients, toss, bring to a simmer and cook over medium heat for 30 minutes.

STEP 4
Divide the whole mix between plates and serve.

NUTRITIONAL INFORMATION
Calories 352, Fat 12.7g, Carbs 33.2g, Protein 13.5g

FIVE SPICE CHICKEN BREAST

 Cooking Difficulty: 3/10

 Cooking Time: 26 minutes

 Servings: 4

INGREDIENTS

- black pepper
- 1 tsp. five spice
- 1 tbsps. hot pepper
- 1 tbsp. avocado oil
- 1 tbsp. cilantro, chopped
- 2 chicken breast halves, skinless, deboned, and halved
- 1 c. tomatoes, crushed
- 2 tbsps. coconut aminos

STEP 1
Heat up a pan with the oil over medium heat, add the meat and brown it for 2 minutes on each side.

STEP 2
Add the tomatoes, five spice, and the other ingredients, bring to a simmer, and cook over medium heat for 30 minutes.

STEP 3
Divide the whole mix between plates and serve.

NUTRITIONAL INFORMATION
Calories 244, Fat 8.4g, Carbs 4.5g, Protein 31g

MEATBALLS WITH SPINACH AND SUN-DRIED TOMATOES

 Cooking Difficulty: 3/10

 Cooking Time: 28 minutes

 Servings: 2

INGREDIENTS

- ⅛ tsp. black pepper
- 1 ½ c. chop spinach
- 1 c. sun-dried tomatoes in olive oil
- 1 lb. grass-fed ground beef
- 2 tbsp. coconut oil

STEP 1
With your hands, combine all the ingredients in a big bowl. Shape the meat mixture into patties.

STEP 2
In a frying pan, melt coconut oil over med-high heat.

STEP 3
Adjust heat to medium and continue cooking the patties for 4 to 5 minutes on each side or until cooked through.

STEP 4
Serve.

NUTRITIONAL INFORMATION
340 Calories, 9g Carbs, 24g Protein, 24g Fat

103

CHICKEN AND MUSHROOMS

 Cooking Difficulty: 3/10	Cooking Time: 15 minutes	Servings: 4

INGREDIENTS

- ½ tsp. chili flakes
- 1 tbsp. olive oil
- black pepper
- ½ lb. white mushrooms halved
- 2 tbsps. olive oil
- 2 chicken breasts, skinless, deboned and halved

STEP 1
Heat up a pan with the oil over medium-high heat, add the mushrooms, toss and sauté for 5 minutes.

STEP 2
Add the meat, toss and cook for 5 minutes more.

STEP 3
Add the other ingredients, bring to a simmer and cook over medium heat for 5 minutes.

STEP 4
Divide the mix between plates and serve.

NUTRITIONAL INFORMATION
Calories 455, Fat 6g, Carbs 4g, Protein 13g

SALMON AND SHRIMP BOWLS

 Cooking Difficulty: 2/10

 Cooking Time: 12 minutes

 Servings: 4

INGREDIENTS

- ½ c. mild salsa
- 1 tbsp. olive oil
- ½ lb. shrimp, peeled and deveined
- 1 red onion, chopped
- 2 tbsps. cilantro, chopped
- ½ lb. smoked salmon, skinless, deboned and cubed
- ¼ c. tomatoes, cubed

STEP 1

Heat up a pan with the oil over medium-high heat, add the salmon, toss and cook for 5 minutes.

STEP 2

Add the onion, shrimp, and the other ingredients, cook for 7 minutes more, divide into bowls, and serve.

NUTRITIONAL INFORMATION

Calories 251, Fat 11.4g, Carbs 12.3g, Protein 7.1g

SHRIMP SALAD

Cooking Difficulty: 2/10	Cooking Time: 8 minutes	Servings: 4

INGREDIENTS

- 1 lb. shrimp, deveined and peeled
- 1 red onion, sliced
- ¼ tsp. black pepper
- 2 c. baby arugula
- 1 tbsp. lemon juice
- 1 tbsp. olive oil

STEP 1

Heat up a pan with the oil over medium heat, add the onion, stir and sauté for 2 minutes.

STEP 2

Add the shrimp and the other ingredients, toss, cook for 6 minutes, divide into bowls and serve.

NUTRITIONAL INFORMATION

Calories 341, Fat 11.5g, Carbs 17.3g, Protein 14.3g

CHICKEN THIGHS AND GRAPES MIX

 Cooking Difficulty: 3/10

 Cooking Time: 42 minutes

 Servings: 4

INGREDIENTS

- 2 garlic cloves, chopped
- 1 c. tomatoes, cubed
- 1 yellow onion, sliced
- black pepper
- ¼ c. chicken stock, low-sodium
- 1 lb. chicken thighs
- 1 carrot, cubed
- 1 tbsp. olive oil
- 1 c. green grapes

STEP 1
Grease a baking pan with the oil, arrange the chicken thighs inside, and add the other ingredients on top.

STEP 2
Bake at 390 degrees F for 40 minutes, divide between plates and serve.

NUTRITIONAL INFORMATION
Calories 289, Fat 12.1g, Carbs 10.3g, Protein 33.9g

PORK WITH LEMON AND TOMATO

 Cooking Difficulty: 3/10

 Cooking Time: 300 minutes

 Servings: 4

INGREDIENTS

- ½ tsp. cayenne pepper
- ½ tsp. paprika
- 8 oz. tomato paste
- 1 chopped onion
- 1 jalapeno pepper
- 1 tsp. cumin
- 1 tsp. thyme
- 2 lbs. pork loin
- 2 tbsps. lemon juice
- 2 tsp. chili powder
- 3 tbsps. coconut oil
- 4 minced garlic cloves

STEP 1
Place all the above ingredients in your crockpot.

STEP 2
Set the crockpot on low and cook for five hours.

STEP 3
Shred the pork using two forks.

STEP 4
Serve warm.

NUTRITIONAL INFORMATION
382 Calories, 18g Carbs, 40g Protein, 17g Fat

SNACKS & DESSERTS

CAULIFLOWER BARS

Cooking Difficulty: 3/10	Cooking Time: 32 minutes	Servings: 8

INGREDIENTS

- 1 c. cauliflower florets, chopped
- ¼ tsp. black pepper
- 2 eggs, whisked
- ½ c. low-fat cheddar, shredded
- 2 tsps. baking powder
- 2 c. whole wheat flour
- 1 c. almond milk

STEP 1

In a bowl, combine the flour with the cauliflower and the other ingredients and stir well.

STEP 2

Spread into a baking tray, introduce in the oven, bake at 400 degrees F for 30 minutes, cut into bars and serve as a snack.

NUTRITIONAL INFORMATION

Calories 430, Fat 18.1g, Carbs 54g, Protein 14.5g

LENTILS SPREAD

 Cooking Difficulty: 3/10

 Cooking Time: 15 minutes

 Servings: 4

INGREDIENTS

- 2 garlic cloves, minced
- ½ c. cilantro, chopped
- 14 oz. canned lentils, drained, unsalted, and rinsed
- 1 lemon juice
- 2 tbsps. olive oil

STEP 1

In a blender, combine the lentils with the oil and the other ingredients, pulse well, divide into bowls and serve as a party spread.

NUTRITIONAL INFORMATION

Calories 416, Fat 8.2g, Carbs 60.4g, Protein 25.8g

ROASTED WALNUTS

 Cooking Difficulty: 1/10	Cooking Time: 15 minutes	Servings: 8

INGREDIENTS

- 14 oz. walnuts
- ½ tsp. garlic powder
- 1 tbsp. avocado oil
- ½ tsp. chili powder
- ½ tsp. smoked paprika
- ¼ tsp. cayenne pepper

STEP 1

Spread the walnuts on a lined baking sheet, add the paprika and the other ingredients, toss and bake at 410 degrees F for 15 minutes. Divide into bowls and serve as a snack.

NUTRITIONAL INFORMATION

Calories 311, Fat 29.6g, Carbs 5.3g, Protein 12g

KALE DIP

Cooking Difficulty: 2/10	Cooking Time: 22 minutes	Servings: 4

INGREDIENTS

- 1 tsp. chili powder
- 1 c. coconut cream
- 1 tbsp. olive oil
- ¼ tsp. black pepper
- 1 bunch kale leaves
- 1 shallot, chopped

STEP 1
Heat up a pan with the oil over medium heat, add the shallots, stir and sauté for 4 minutes.

STEP 2
Add the kale and the other ingredients, bring to a simmer, and cook over medium heat for 16 minutes.

STEP 3
Blend using an immersion blender, divide into bowls and serve as a snack.

NUTRITIONAL INFORMATION
Calories 188, Fat 17.9g, Carbs 7.6g, Protein 2.5g

BEETS CHIPS

 Cooking Difficulty: 2/10

 Cooking Time: 37 minutes

 Servings: 4

INGREDIENTS

- 1 tbsp. olive oil
- 2 tsps. garlic, minced
- 2 beets, peeled and thinly sliced
- 1 tsp. cumin, ground

STEP 1

Spread the beet chips on a lined baking sheet, add the oil and the other ingredients, toss, introduce in the oven and bake at 400 degrees F for 35 minutes.

STEP 2

Divide into bowls and serve as a snack.

NUTRITIONAL INFORMATION
Calories 32, Fat 0.7g, Carbs 6.1g, Protein 1.1g

ZUCCHINI DIP

Cooking Difficulty: 2/10	Cooking Time: 12 minutes	Servings: 4

INGREDIENTS

- 2 spring onions, chopped
- ¼ c. veggie stock, low-sodium
- ¼ tsp. nutmeg, ground
- 2 garlic cloves, minced
- 2 zucchinis, chopped
- 1 tbsp. olive oil
- ½ c. yogurt, nonfat
- 1 tbsp. dill, chopped

STEP 1
Heat up a pan with the oil over medium heat, add the onions and garlic, stir and sauté for 3 minutes.

STEP 2
Add the zucchinis and the other ingredients except the yogurt, toss, cook for 7 minutes more and take off the heat.

STEP 3
Add the yogurt, blend using an immersion blender, divide into bowls, and serve.

NUTRITIONAL INFORMATION
Calories 76, Fat 4.1, Carbs 7.2, Protein 3.4

APPLE DANDELION GREEN SMOOTHIE

 Cooking Difficulty: 1/10	Cooking Time: 1 minutes	Servings: 1

INGREDIENTS

- 4 c. dandelion greens
- ½ c. cranberries, frozen
- 1 peeled banana
- 1 cored apple
- 1 cored pear
- 8 oz. filtered water

STEP 1

Using a blender, set in all your ingredients and process until creamy and smooth. Serve right away!

NUTRITIONAL INFORMATION
Calories: 425, Fat: 3 g, Carbs: 96 g, Protein: 9 g

RAINBOW FRUIT SALAD

Cooking Difficulty: 1/10	Cooking Time: 5 minutes	Servings: 4

INGREDIENTS

for the fruit salad:
- 1 lb. hulled strawberries, sliced
- 1 c. kiwis, halved, cubed
- 1 ¼ c. blueberries
- 1 1/3 c. blackberries
- 1 c. pineapple chunks

for the maple lime dressing:
- 2 tsps. lime zest
- ¼ c. maple syrup
- 1 tbsp. lime juice

STEP 1
Prepare the salad, and for this, take a bowl, place all its ingredients and toss until mixed.

STEP 2
Prepare the dressing, and for this, take a small bowl, place all its ingredients and whisk well.

STEP 3
Drizzle the dressing over salad, toss until coated and serve.

NUTRITIONAL INFORMATION
Calories: 88.1, Fat: 0.4 g, Carbs: 22.6 g, Protein: 1.1 g

APRICOT AND ALMOND CRISP

Cooking Difficulty: 3/10	Cooking Time: 27 minutes	Servings: 4

INGREDIENTS

- 1 tsp. anise seeds
- 1 lb. apricots halved and pitted
- 1 tbsp. oats, gluten-free
- 2 tbsps. honey
- 1 tsp. olive oil
- ½ c. almonds, chopped

STEP 1
Switch on the oven and set it to 350 degrees F to preheat.

STEP 2
Grease a 9inch pie plate with olive oil.

STEP 3
Add chopped apricots to the plate and spread evenly.

STEP 4
Top them with almonds, anise seeds, and oats.

STEP 5
Pour honey on top and bake for 25 minutes until golden brown. Serve.

NUTRITIONAL INFORMATION
Calories 149, Fat 11.9 , Carbs 18.8 , Protein 3

CRISPY BAKED APPLE

 Cooking Difficulty: 2/10	Cooking Time: 120 minutes	Servings: 2

INGREDIENTS

- 1 tsp. cinnamon sugar
- 2 apples

STEP 1

Pre-heat your oven to 200 degrees Fahrenheit. Use a knife to carefully slice the apples thinly. Remove the seeds.

STEP 2

Use parchment paper in the baking sheet and arrange the apple slices make sure that it will not overlap each other.

STEP 3

Sprinkle cinnamon sugar on top of the apple.

STEP 4

Bake for one hour, then flip. Bake for another hour, flip occasionally until all the apple slices are dry.

NUTRITIONAL INFORMATION

35 Calories, 10g Carbs, 0g Protein, 0g Fat

APPLE AVOCADO SMOOTHIE

 Cooking Difficulty: 1/10	Cooking Time: 1 minutes	Servings: 1

INGREDIENTS

- 1 tbsp. freshly squeezed lime juice
- ½ avocado
- 1 green apple
- 1 c. water

STEP 1

Using a blender, set in all your ingredients and process until creamy and smooth. Serve right away!

NUTRITIONAL INFORMATION
Calories: 233, Fat: 15 g, Carbs: 28 g, Protein: 2.4 g

APPLE KALE SMOOTHIE

 Cooking Difficulty: 1/10

 Cooking Time: 1 minutes

 Servings: 1

INGREDIENTS

- 1 tbsp. lemon juice, freshly squeezed
- ½ c. apple juice, freshly extracted
- ½ banana
- 1 stalk celery, chopped
- ¾ c. chopped kale, stemmed
- ½ c. ice

STEP 1

Using a blender, set in all your ingredients and process well until very smooth. Serve immediately.

NUTRITIONAL INFORMATION
Calories: 139, Fat: 1 g, Carbs: 35 g, Protein: 3 g

CHOCOLATE PEANUT BUTTER ENERGY BITES

 Cooking Difficulty: 1/10

 Cooking Time: 4 minutes

 Servings: 4

INGREDIENTS

- ½ c. oats, old-fashioned
- 1/3 c. cocoa powder, unsweetened
- 1 c. dates, chopped
- ½ c. shredded coconut flakes, unsweetened
- ½ c. peanut butter

STEP 1
Place oats in a food processor along with dates and pulse for 1 minute until the paste starts to come together.

STEP 2
Then add remaining ingredients, and blend until incorporated and very thick mixture comes together.

STEP 3
Shape the mixture into balls, refrigerate for 1 hour until set and then serve.

NUTRITIONAL INFORMATION
Calories: 88.6, Fat: 5 g, Carbs: 10 g, Protein: 2.3 g

SIMPLE BANANA COOKIES

Cooking Difficulty: 2/10	Cooking Time: 16 minutes	Servings: 4

INGREDIENTS

- 3 tbsps. peanut butter
- 3 bananas
- ¼ c. walnuts
- 1 c. rolled oats

STEP 1

For a simple but delicious cookie, start by prepping the oven to 350. As the oven warms up, take out your mixing bowl and first mash the bananas before adding in the oats.

STEP 2

When you have folded the oats in, add in the walnuts and peanut butter before using your hands to layout small balls onto a baking sheet. Once this is set, pop the dish into the oven for fifteen minutes and bake your cookies.

STEP 3

By the end of fifteen minutes, remove the dish from the oven and allow them to cool for five minutes before enjoying.

NUTRITIONAL INFORMATION
Calories: 250, Carbs: 30g, Fats: 10g, Proteins: 5g

CONCLUSION

In conclusion, «Effortless DASH Diet Cookbook» is not just a recipe collection but a comprehensive guide for those striving for a healthier lifestyle. The DASH diet proves to be an effective tool for controlling blood pressure and improving overall health. This book offers a variety of flavorful and nutritious recipes to make your transition to healthy eating more enjoyable and exciting.

We have discussed the principles of the DASH diet, including limiting sodium intake, increasing consumption of nutrient-rich foods, and maintaining a calorie balance. These simple yet essential steps can lead to improved well-being, reduced risk of cardiovascular diseases, and enhanced quality of life.

Remember that success in adopting the DASH diet and achieving your health goals depends on your commitment and perseverance. Start slowly, try new recipes, and gradually incorporate healthy habits into your daily life.

Let «Effortless DASH Diet Cookbook» be your trusted guide on this exciting journey to health and well-being.

Eva Evans

Made in the USA
Las Vegas, NV
29 March 2025